Basic Accounting

for

Small

Groups

John
Cammack

Oxfam (UK and Ireland)

Published by Oxfam (UK and Ireland)

First published in 1992 Reprinted in 1996

ISBN 0 85598 148 2

© Oxfam (UK and Ireland) 1992

A catologue record for this book is available from the British Library.

Cover photos:
Village pharmacy, Burkina Faso (Jeremy Hartley/Oxfam)
Coffee growers' co-operative, Haiti (Caroline Watson/Oxfam)

Published by Oxfam (UK and Ireland), 274 Banbury Road, Oxford OX2 7DZ, UK; tel. (0)1865 313922; e-mail publish@oxfam.org.uk

(registered as a charity, no. 202918)

Available from the following agents:
for *Canada and the USA*: Humanities Press International, 165 First Avenue, Atlantic Highlands, New Jersey NJ 07716-1289, USA; tel. (908) 872 1441; fax (908) 872 0717
for *southern Africa*: David Philip Publishers, PO Box 23408, Claremont, Cape Town 7735, South Africa; tel. (021) 64 4136; fax (021) 64 3358.

Available in Ireland from Oxfam in Ireland, 19 Clanwilliam Terrace, Dublin 2 (tel. 01 661 8544).

Designed by Oxfam Design Department
Printed by Oxfam Print Unit

Oxfam (UK and Ireland) is a member of Oxfam International.

CONTENTS

FOREWORD

The thought of taking on the responsibility for keeping accounting records fills many people with horror. 'What does it all mean?'... 'What do I do with all these figures?'... 'Where do I start?' are common reactions. But proper financial control can be the key to the success of a venture, whatever its size. And the basic principles, being logical and consistent, are not difficult to apply once they have been explained.

If you are running a small group or project without any experience of keeping accounts, this book is for you. It should help you to understand the basic rules and put them into practice with confidence. More detailed accounting information will be needed in some cases, if (for example) you need to calculate profits in a trading operation. Such information is beyond the scope of this book; but if you have no other help, at least the system explained here will keep your records in order.

No currency has been quoted in any of the examples in the book, because (we hope) it will be used in a number of countries, with various currencies.

This book is the result of seven years' experience of working on financial record-keeping with Oxfam's overseas offices and projects. But the procedures that it describes are not specific to Oxfam, or even to development projects. It should be useful to any small group that needs to keep accurate records of its financial transactions.

ACKNOWLEDGEMENTS

I would like to thank those members of Oxfam's staff, past and present, who have encouraged me to write this book, and who have made helpful suggestions. In particular, thanks are due to Gopal Rao, Peter Howlett, and Stephen Lloyd, and to those associated with Oxfam's project partners and overseas offices who have shared their experiences with me. Also thanks to Freda, my wife, for reading through the early versions and testing out the material as a true non-accountant!

John Cammack
Oxford
May 1992

1 INTRODUCTION: WHY KEEP ACCOUNTS?

Clear accounting maintains friendship.
(Nicaraguan proverb)

All small projects need clear accounting, for a number of reasons:

- All members of the group need to know what money is available and how it has been spent.
- Accounting is often required by law. Even if it is not, the people who have given money to the group need to know how it has been used.
- The information provided by clear accounts is valuable in running the group.
- It 'maintains friendship', by showing that the person responsible for keeping the accounts is honest.

The aim of this guide is to help you to maintain records of money coming in and going out; to show you how to make use of the information provided; and to show how to prepare a summary of the way in which the money has been used.

Northern Tanzania: a women's group near Moshi has set up a cattle-dipping enterprise. Here, Paulina Gideon Natennna, of the Maasai Health Services Project, advises Natangadwaki Kisota, one of three co-signatories of the bank account. *(Geoff Sayer/Oxfam)*

2 DECIDING WHAT YOUR PROJECT WILL COST

The first stage in keeping accounts for a small project comes before any money has been spent! It is the stage when you decide what you want to do, and how much it will cost.

Establishing your plans

Firstly, you need to decide your objectives – that is to say, what you want to achieve. This is not something that the person responsible for the accounts can do alone. As far as possible, every member of the group needs to be involved in the discussion, so that they will feel committed to what happens.

The next stage should also be discussed with the entire group. This is to decide what is needed in order to achieve these objectives; for example:

- How many people will be needed?
- Will they need to travel?
- What materials are required?
- Will premises be needed?

Then decide what these items will cost. Some of these costs will be obvious, but others will not. Sometimes you will need to talk with merchants or suppliers to get estimates of the cost of materials. You should choose the most appropriate estimate (which will not necessarily be the lowest).

After you have gathered together all the costs, you need to write them down on paper, item by item. It is important at this stage to make sure that each type of cost is written down separately, as shown in Figure 1 on the next page. This listing is called a **budget.**

How to construct a budget

The budget should include not only items of costs (also called **payments, expenses,** or **expenditure**), but also money that you know (or are fairly certain) you will receive. It should always be for a fixed period of time; for example, a year.

When you apply for money from a donor, you will need to give them your proposed budget, which will exclude the amount you hope they will fund. Let's look at an example of a budget. Figure 1 relates to a primary health care programme, but the same rules apply to all budgets.

BUDGET FOR PRIMARY HEALTH CARE PROGRAMME
FOR THE PERIOD 1 JANUARY 19– TO 31 DECEMBER 19–

Money coming in	
Grant from donor	19000
Grant from Department of Health	28000
Miscellaneous sales	600
Total	47600
Money going out	
Salaries	12000
Rent of premises	5000
Purchase of drugs	10000
Other medical supplies	17600
Electricity	1000
Other expenses	2000
Total	47600

Figure 1: Example of a budget

We will go through Figure 1 item by item to see how the budget was made.

Grants

This budget assumes that the grants have already been agreed. There may be a stage before this when, for example, the Department of Health has definitely promised a grant, but the grant from the other donor is uncertain. If so, either it should be excluded from the budget, or a note should be written at the side of the item, to say that it is not guaranteed.

Miscellaneous sales

There will be some sales of drugs or other medical supplies. It is always difficult to estimate how many sales there will be – particularly with medical programmes, as you do not know who will be ill! The only way to estimate is to take your best guess, and try not to be too optimistic.

Salaries

Calculate the number of people working on the project, and the amount paid to them. Remember to include any extra costs, such as insurance and government taxes.

Rent of premises

If you have a building already in mind, the rent can be agreed with the owner. If there is no suitable building available, find out what a similar building is likely to cost. Include these figures in the budget.

Purchase of drugs and other medical supplies

These are both large items in the budget. Ask for written estimates from several suppliers.

Electricity

Ask other people in your area about the level of charges locally for items such as electricity and water (if available).

Other expenses

Although only one figure is included in the budget, it covers a number of different items, such as post, telephone, stationery, and travel costs. A list of these is needed to support the budget.

Remember that costs may rise from the time you prepare your budget to the time when you spend the money. Try to allow for this in your calculations.

BUDGET FOR PRIMARY HEALTH CARE PROGRAMME: 1 January to 31 December 19—

Item	Jan	Feb	Mar	Apr	May	Jun	July	Aug	Sept	Oct	Nov	Dec	Total
Money coming in													
Grant from donor	9500	–	–	–	–	–	9500	–	–	–	–	–	19000
Grant from Dept. of Health	14000	–	–	–	–	–	14000	–	–	–	–	–	28000
Miscellaneous sales	50	50	50	50	50	50	50	50	50	50	50	50	600
Total	23550	50	50	50	50	50	23550	50	50	50	50	50	47600
Cumulative total	23550	23600	23650	23700	23750	23800	47350	47400	47450	47500	47550	47600	–
Money going out													
Salaries	1000	1000	1000	1000	1000	1000	1000	1000	1000	1000	1000	1000	12000
Rent of premises	417	417	417	417	417	417	417	417	416	416	416	416	5000
Purchase of drugs	5000	–	–	–	–	–	5000	–	–	–	–	–	10000
Other medical supplies	4400	–	–	4400	–	–	4400	–	–	4400	–	–	17600
Electricity	83	83	83	83	83	83	83	83	84	84	84	84	1000
Other expenses	167	167	167	167	167	167	167	167	166	166	166	166	2000
Total	11067	1667	1667	6067	1667	1667	11067	1667	1666	6066	1666	1666	47600
Cumulative total	11067	12734	14401	20468	22135	23802	34869	36536	38202	44268	45934	47600	–

Figure 2: Budget broken down over 12 months

Breaking down the budget

The next stage of preparing the budget is to decide how much money will come in and go out in each individual month. Figure 2 (opposite) gives an example of how this breakdown looks, using the information in Figure 1. There are two reasons for presenting the budget in this way:

- It helps you to monitor spending month by month. (We will look at this again in Chapter 8.)
- It shows whether or not you will have enough money coming in to pay for what is going out. This is why the **cumulative total** is shown. By cumulative, we mean the total for the current month, added to the total for the previous months.

The cumulative balances can be used to show the times of the year when you are likely to run out of money.

Month	Cumulative money coming in	Cumulative money going out	Difference
January	23550	11067	12483
February	23600	12734	10866
March	23650	14401	9249
April	23700	20468	3232
May	23750	22135	1615
June	23800	23802	(2)
July	47350	34869	12481
August	47400	36536	10864
September	47450	38202	9248
October	47500	44268	3232
November	47550	45934	1616
December	47600	47600	0

Figure 3: Comparison of cumulative balances

In the example shown in Figure 3, the months leading up to June and December (just before more money comes in) are ones where you may run out of funds. To avoid problems, you may have to say that you cannot afford to pay for purchases when planned, or ask the people giving you money to pay earlier. Maybe you will need to arrange a temporary loan.

Whatever the situation, and whether or not you need to do anything about it, you will know in advance from a breakdown like the one shown in Figures 2 and 3. This is called a **cash flow forecast** or **cash budget**.

Whenever funds are requested from a voluntary agency or government department, or if a bank loan is necessary, it is important to back up your request with a budget and a cash flow forecast.

Towards the end of each year, you will need to prepare a similar budget and cash flow forecast for the next financial year. When you are preparing it for the second time, you will have gained valuable experience in what is likely to happen, and how much items cost.

You must keep referring back to these as the year progresses. Sometimes you will need to revise the figures. If you do, always tell the people who have given you money. It is helpful to prepare a budget for one or two years in advance. Sometimes the people giving you funds will ask for this.

Budgets and price increases

Because budgets are prepared in advance, price increases may affect items in your budget even before you start to spend! This is often referred to as **inflation**. These increases happen in most countries, and you will be aware from your own personal finances what this means. There are no simple solutions to dealing with it!

You should build into your budget an amount to cover possible increases. You will have different categories of price increases:

- *Items that are likely to increase in price.* If you do not know what the increase is likely to be, the rate of past changes will give you a guide. There may be a government forecast of how prices will increase. Use this with care, as most governments will be over-optimistic! It is far better to use your own best estimate.
- *Salaries* are difficult to estimate, as any increase in them will depend on the general level of price increases. Unless you have already agreed on salary increases for the following year, you will have to put your best estimate in the budget. But such guesses can lead to trouble: staff may assume that it will be a reality!

- *Items to be purchased at a fixed price:* if you have already agreed a price with a supplier, you should include that figure in the budget.
- *Increase in income:* Remember that if inflation occurs, you may also increase your fees and charges. Build this into your income budget.

However you calculate the budget items, it is essential to keep a record of your working figures which can be shown to donors. This is especially important if you get it wrong! Donors may be willing to consider giving you a supplementary grant, *but only if you can show how the original budget was calculated, and what has happened to change it.*

Summary of this chapter

- Establish your objectives, and involve everyone in the decisions.
- Decide what is needed to fulfil these objectives.
- Work out the costs, with help from other people.
- Write them down, item by item, for a fixed period of time.
- Write down the details of money coming in and money going out month by month.
- Use the budget and the cash flow forecast when applying for funds.
- Prepare a similar budget for each year.
- When an increase in prices is likely to occur, include these costs in the budget, and keep a record of all your calculations.

3 RECORDS OF MONEY COMING IN AND GOING OUT

One of the most important rules in keeping accounts is to *make sure that everything is written down, and that every piece of paper is kept.* However, without any previous experience of keeping accounts it is difficult to know how to write things down. This chapter will show you the way to do it.

Recording the money

First of all, you can divide the finances of your group into two parts: money coming in, and money going out. You will need a book to use only for this purpose. It is called a **cash book,** because it records money or cash coming in and going out. You can either buy a special cash book with lines already drawn, or use an exercise book and draw your own lines, as shown in Figure 4.

This page is then ready for you to write down any money that comes in or goes out of the group, the date when it happens, what it is, how much it is, and (in the balance column) how much cash is left.

Date	Details	Cash amount IN	Cash amount OUT	Balance

Figure 4: Layout of a cash book

Figure 5 gives an example. This example, and others that follow, assume that the group had some cash available to use at the beginning of the month. This is referred to as **cash in hand**.

CASH BOOK

Date	Details	Cash amount IN	Cash amount OUT	Balance
1 Jan	Cash in hand	1000.00		1000.00
3 Jan	Grant from donor	9500.00		10500.00
3 Jan	Stationery for office		10.00	10490.00
5 Jan	Purchase of medical supplies		650.00	9840.00
7 Jan	Driver's salary		200.00	9640.00
7 Jan	Purchase of drugs		3450.00	6190.00
9 Jan	Grant from Dept. of Health	7000.00		13190.00
9 Jan	Sale of drugs	14.50		13204.50

Figure 5: Example of a completed cash book

Figure 5 shows a record of cash coming in and going out, but also the balance of cash after each entry has been included. This is important, because it shows how much cash you should have left, and lets you count the actual cash to make sure it agrees with the cash book. The cash must be counted regularly. If it does not agree, it may be that you have forgotten to write something down (a mistake which you can correct), or (more seriously) that some money may have been lost or stolen. If so, it is essential to know this as soon as possible.

We said earlier that it is important to write everything down when keeping accounts, and that every piece of paper relating to money is kept. We will now look at the pieces of paper you are likely to need.

Payment receipts

When you pay an amount from your cash, for example the driver's salary in Figure 5, you could just hand over the money. However, one day, the driver might claim that s/he was not paid. Although you may be certain that you did pay the salary, there would be no written proof of this.

To avoid this situation arising, every time you pay a salary, or indeed any other item, you must ask the person receiving the money to sign, or make their mark/thumbprint, for it. This signed piece of paper is called a **receipt**. All receipts must be kept together in a separate file. Figure 6 shows an example of a receipt.

```
┌─────────────────────────────────────────────────────────┐
│  (Name of Organisation)        Receipt Number _____       │
│                                                           │
│  Date _____          Amount _____        │
│                                                           │
│  Received from _____  │
│                                                           │
│  Description _____  │
│                                                           │
│  _____  │
│                                                           │
│  Received by _____  │
│                                                           │
└─────────────────────────────────────────────────────────┘
```

Figure 6: Example of a receipt

Each receipt should be numbered, and its number put against the entry in the cash book, as shown in Figure 7. It is then easier to find it if you need it.

If any other paperwork (such as a request for payment from a merchant or supplier – called an **invoice**) is available, this too should be attached to the receipt and filed. In the future you or someone else will be able to find out from this paperwork exactly what happened.

Income receipts

In the same way, when people give money to your group, they will want a receipt from you to prove that they have handed over the money. Even if they do not ask for one, it is good practice to give them one. You will need to keep a duplicate copy of this, which must be filed on an income receipts file.

The format can be the same as the payment receipt, but it is helpful to identify them in some way – perhaps by a different colour – and to have a different sequence of receipt numbers for each. These numbers should also be put in the cash book for reference.

Unfortunately, the word 'receipts' has two meanings! Firstly, it means these signed pieces of paper. But secondly, accountants and book-keepers use it to mean *money coming in*. It has a similar meaning to 'income'. When the word 'receipts' is used for money coming in, the word used for money going out is 'payments'.

From now on, we will use the words 'receipts' and 'payments' to describe money coming in and going out. The cash book will then look like the example in Figure 7. (Note that the cash in hand is already a part of the cash, so it has no receipt number.)

CASH BOOK

Date	Detail	Receipt number	Receipts (cash in) amount	Payments (cash out) amount	Balance
1 Jan	Cash in hand	—	1000.00		1000.00
3 Jan	Grant from donor	500	9500.00		10500.00
3 Jan	Stationery for office	1		10.00	10490.00
5 Jan	Purchase of medical supplies	2		650.00	9840.00
7 Jan	Driver's salary	3		200.00	9640.00
7 Jan	Purchase of drugs	4		3450.00	6190.00
9 Jan	Grant from Dept of Health	501	7000.00		13190.00
9 Jan	Sale of drugs	502	14.50		13204.50

Figure 7: Example of a cash book with receipt numbers

Another method of presentation

Receipts and payments may be shown on separate pages of the cash book, which would look like the example in Figure 8 on the next page.

This needs more space in your book, but it means that no balancing figure is shown. To find the balance (at any time), you need to add up all the payment amounts, and subtract this total from the total of all the receipts amounts. You can then draw a line (as shown in Figure 8), and write down the totals, and the balance.

CASH BOOK

	RECEIPTS				PAYMENTS		
Date	**Detail**	**Receipt number**	**Amount**	**Date**	**Details**	**Receipt number**	**Amount**
1 Jan	Cash in hand		1000.00	3 Jan	Stationery for office	1	10.00
3 Jan	Grant from donor	500	9500.00	5 Jan	Purchase of medical supplies	2	650.00
9 Jan	Grant from Dept. of Health	501	7000.00	7 Jan	Driver's salary	3	200.00
9 Jan	Sale of drugs	502	14.50	7 Jan	Purchase of drugs	4	3450.00
9 Jan	Total		17514.50	9 Jan	Total		4310.00
					Balance (9 Jan)		13204.50

Figure 8: Example of a cash book with receipts and payments shown separately

Whichever way the cash book is presented, a total of the cash balance needs to be shown at the end of each month. This should always be the same as the cash actually held.

At the beginning of each month, start a new page in your cash book, and write in the 'cash in hand', which is the balance at the end of the previous month. Sometimes people describe this as the **balance brought forward** (or **balance b/f**).

Rules to help you to control your cash

So far, we have looked at accounting for money, but not at the actual cash itself (that is, the notes and coins). There are a few rules to make your cash control much easier:

1 *Always keep your cash secure*, preferably in a lockable tin, which is kept in a safe or locked cupboard.
2 *Make sure that only one person is responsible for the cash.* Whenever this person changes, let the outgoing person and the incoming person count the cash and agree the amount together. This should be written down and signed by both.
3 *Ideally, the person responsible for the cash should be a different person from the one keeping the accounts.*
4 *Someone in a senior position* within the group (for example, the project or group leader) *should count the cash regularly*, and agree the figure with the cash book. This helps the person looking after the cash, as s/he is shown to be honest.
5 *A senior person should also authorise any large or unusual payments.* You may like to set a limit, beyond which the person handling the money should obtain (written) approval for expenditure.
6 *Always issue receipts for any cash received or paid*, and make an entry in the cash book.
7 In some countries it is possible to *obtain insurance to cover the holding of cash*. If amounts are large, it is worth considering this. (If you do, don't forget to include the premium in your budget!)
8 You should always *know in advance how much cash you are likely to need*. Don't wait until the time you need to pay someone before realising that you have no money left.
9 *If your project's money is running out, take action as soon as possible.*

Summary of this chapter

- Keep all documents relating to the accounts.
- Open a cash book to record money coming in (receipts) and money going out (payments).
- Record all details as you go along.
- Remember that the word 'receipts' has two meanings: one relates to money received, the other relates to the piece of paper saying that an amount of money has changed hands.
- Have numbered receipts available to be signed by people to whom you give money, and for you to sign when you are given money.
- File receipts for receipts and for payments separately, along with any other relevant paperwork.
- Include the receipt numbers in your cash book as a reference.
- Count the cash regularly, and agree the total with the figure in your cash book.

• Make sure that you use the rules to control your cash.

For very small groups, this will be enough to record what is happening to the cash. The next chapter will show you a way of arranging the information in a more useful order for groups which have more than, say, twenty or thirty entries in the cash book each month.

4 ARRANGING YOUR RECORDS TO GIVE MORE INFORMATION

If you have read Chapter 3, and you think that the way of completing a cash book shown there is sufficient for your group, there is no need to read this chapter. However, if you want to extract more information, or if you just want to make sure you are not missing anything, then read on!

One of the problems with the cash book which we looked at in Chapter 3 is that, although it will tell you exactly what cash has come in and gone out, and the balance of cash left (all of which is very useful), it does not tell you anything *about* the money.

The analysed cash book

You will need to know, for example, how much refers to income from grants, rather than income from sales, and how much has been spent on salaries, rather than on purchase of medicines. With only a few entries in the cash book, you can easily add them up. However with more and more entries, you need to have a system to help. This is done in an **analysed cash book,** which means that in addition to the cash book columns which we saw in the last chapter, there are extra columns which show the *type* of money it is. More space will be required when completing an analysed cash book, so you need either to rule up a larger book, or to buy a book ready ruled.

Let us look at an example, using the same figures as we used in the last chapter. Because of lack of space here, we will first look at the receipts side (Figure 9), and then at the payments side (Figure 10).

ANALYSED CASH BOOK							
Receipts							
Date	Details	Receipt number	Amount	Balance b/f	Grants	Sale of drugs	Other
1 Jan	Cash in hand	—	1000.00	1000.00			
3 Jan	Grant from donor	500	9500.00		9500.00		
9 Jan	Grant from Dept. of Health	501	7000.00		7000.00		
9 Jan	Sale of drugs	502	14.50			14.50	
31 Jan	Total		17514.50	1000.00	16500.00	14.50	—

Figure 9: Receipts side of an analysed cash book

A few points to note from the analysed cash book:

• The figure received or paid is always listed in the amount column *and then again in one of the other columns.*
• *The headings are the same as those included in the budget.* This will help when you compare the actual figures with the budgeted figures.
• There is an extra column on both the receipts side and the payments side, which is called 'other'. This is useful in practice, because items arise which do not fall under any one heading. If an item does appear here, we may well want to question why it was spent, as it was not included in the budget.
• At the end of the month, we need to *add up all the columns.* The total of all the analysed receipts columns (ignoring the amount column) should add up to the total of the receipts amount column. (In Figure 9, for example, 1000.00 + 16500.00 + 14.50 = 17514.50.) If not, you have entered something in the wrong place! (Remember you have entered each item twice.)
• Similarly, the total of all the analysed payments columns (other than the amount column) should add up to the total of the payments amount column. (In Figure 10, for example, 200.00 + 3450.00 + 650.00 + 10.00 = 4310.00.)
• The cash balance can be obtained by *subtracting the total of the payments amount column from the total of the receipts amount column.*

ANALYSED CASH BOOK
Payments

Date	Details	Receipt number	Amount	Salaries	Rent	Drugs	Medical supplies	Electricity	Other expenses	Other
3 Jan	Stationery for office	1	10.00						10.00	–
5 Jan	Purchase of medical supplies	2	650.00				650.00			
7 Jan	Driver's salary	3	200.00	200.00						
7 Jan	Purchase of drugs	4	3450.00			3450.00				
31 Jan	Total		4310.00	200.00	–	3450.00	650.00	–	10.00	–

Figure 10: Payments side of an analysed cash book

Summary of this chapter

- An analysed cash book will be useful if you have more than twenty or thirty entries in your cash book each month. It will give you more details of the money you have received and paid.
- You will need more space for this, and it is easier if the receipts and payments are on separate pages.
- Each part will have an amount column, and analysis columns drawn up using the headings from the budget.
- The amount received or paid is always entered twice: once in the amount column, and once in an analysis column.
- The total of the receipts amount column will be equal to the total of all the receipts analysis columns. This will also be the case for payments.

5 BANK ACCOUNTS

As any group grows, there comes a point when it can no longer rely on cash for everything, but also needs to use a bank account.

What the bank will offer

Most banks can operate several kinds of account for you.

Current accounts

This is the most common type of account. You can pay money in, and write cheques to make payments from it, as often as you like (as long as there is enough money in the account!). Sometimes it is possible to take more money out than you have in the account; this is called an **overdraft**. It can only be done with the agreement of the bank, and you will have to pay to do it; the charge is called **interest**.

Banks will often make a charge for operating your account (called a **bank charge**). They will not usually pay you interest on a current account.

Deposit accounts

If you have money which you do not need for some time, it can be placed in a deposit account. The bank will pay you interest for holding the money, but you will usually have to tell the bank in advance if you want the money repaid. Your bank may also offer you a savings account, paying a different rate of interest from a deposit account, possibly with extra restrictions. Sometimes the deposit and savings accounts are the same.

How to account for bank accounts

Accounting for your money at the bank is similar to accounting for cash. But instead of a cash book you need a **bank book**. This is your record of your money at the bank, and it should be kept accurately.

You can buy a bank book, or draw lines in an exercise book, as we did with the cash book. It is useful to have separate pages for money going into the account, and money coming out of it. Figure 11 shows an example.

If you have more than one bank account (for example, a current and a deposit account), it is important to keep a separate bank book, or separate pages in the same bank book, for each account.

BANK BOOK
Receipts

Date	Details	Paying-in reference	Amount
10 Jan	Cash (grant paid in)	856	7000.00
10 Jan	Sale of drugs	857	20.00
12 Jan	Sale of medical supplies	858	127.00
			7147.00

Payments

Date	Details	Receipt number	Cheque number	Amount
10 Jan	Rent of premises	5	1701	2500.00
11 Jan	Medical supplies	6	1702	3000.00
16 Jan	Purchase of drugs	7	1703	550.00
27 Jan	Office equipment	8	1704	100.00
				6150.00

Figure 11: Example of entries in a bank book

As with the cash book, we can obtain the balance at the bank by subtracting the payments total from the receipts total. In this case the bank balance will be 7147.00 − 6150.00 = 997.00.

Transfers between bank and cash

When cash is paid into the bank account, or when a cheque is written for cash, this will affect your cash book and your bank book. If you pay cash into the bank, your cash balance will decrease, and your bank balance will increase. So your cash and bank books will look like Figure 12.

	CASH BOOK Payments				BANK BOOK Receipts		
Date	Details	Receipt number	Cash amount	Date	Details	Paying-in reference	Bank amount
29 Dec	Cash to bank	—	400.00	29 Dec	Cash to bank	855	400.00

Figure 12: Entries in your records when cash is paid into the bank

If you decide that your cash is low, and you wish to withdraw money from your bank account, your bank balance will decrease, and your cash balance will increase. So your cash and bank books will look like Figure 13.

	BANK BOOK Payments					CASH BOOK Receipts		
Date	Details	Receipt number	Cheque number	Bank amount	Date	Details	Receipt number	Cash amount
30 Dec	Bank to cash	—	1699	600.00	30 Dec	Bank to cash	—	600.00

Figure 13: Entries in your records when cash is withdrawn from the bank

Always remember to make entries in both your cash and bank books, if you pay cash into the bank, or take cash out of the bank.

Points to remember when filling in your bank book

1 The receipts in your bank book will be either money that you yourself have paid into the bank, or amounts that have been paid directly into your account by someone else. Any paperwork connected with this should be filed in order, and given a reference number (the paying-in reference in Figures 11 and 12). This reference will help if there are any future queries.

2 The bank may give you a **bank paying-in book** with which to pay cash and cheques into your account. Each form has two copies, one for the bank and a duplicate copy for you to keep. If the bank does not give you a special book, it will provide paying-in slips for this purpose, and you should retain a record of the slip, which the bank should initial. This is proof that you have paid the money in. The slip should be filed according to the paying-in reference order.

3 The bank will give you details of amounts that appear on your bank statement which you have not paid in yourself. It is useful to follow the sequence of paying-in reference numbers for filing paperwork, although this will be at a later date.

4 The payments part of your bank book also includes a column for a receipt number. You may ask the person receiving a cheque to sign a receipt (as you should in the case of cash). However, it is not so important to obtain a receipt for cheque payments. Many large organisations do not bother with receipts for payment by cheque. However, it is useful to have the 'receipt number' reference, whether or not receipts are received. All paperwork (for example invoices) can then be filed in order of the receipt numbers.

5 Each time a payment is made, the number (or the last three or four digits) of the cheque should be recorded in the bank book.

Two other methods of presentation

It is possible to arrange the bank book in an analysed format, as shown with the cash book in Chapter 4. Extra columns would be needed to record the paying-in references and cheque numbers.

Another possible presentation would be to combine the cash and bank book columns into one book. The column headings would then look like Figure 14. This method looks slightly more complicated than keeping separate books, but it means that all similar information is kept in one place. Use whichever presentation you are happiest with.

CASH AND BANK BOOK
Receipts

Date	Details	Receipt number	Paying-in reference	Cash amount	Bank amount

Payments

Date	Details	Receipt number	Cheque number	Cash amount	Bank amount

Figure 14: Headings of a combined cash and bank book

Ensuring that your figures are the same as the bank's

The bank will let you know how much money they think you have in your account. This will be shown in either a **bank pass book** or a **bank statement.** Bank statements tend to be more widely used, especially for current accounts.

Whenever you receive a bank statement, or have your bank pass book brought up to date, you must make sure that your bank book figures are the same as the bank's. This is called a **reconciliation** or **bank reconciliation.** *Do this regularly.* The details you have available will be something like the example shown in Figure 15 (page 26).

You need to go through a number of stages to make sure that your bank book and the bank statement (pass book) reconcile:

1 Enter any outstanding items in your bank book.
2 Include any charges or interest from the bank statement in your bank book.
3 Tick off the items that appear in your bank book and in the bank's records.
4 Construct a table to show how the two records agree. Use all items that are not ticked off. The form should look like Figure 16.

If you do not agree, check your figures again. If you still do not agree, it is worth checking the adding up on your statement/pass book: banks do sometimes make mistakes!

BANK BOOK

Receipts

Date	Details	Paying-in reference	Amount
10 Jan	Cash to bank	856	7000.00
10 Jan	Sale of drugs	857	20.00
12 Jan	Sale of medical supplies	858	127.00
			7147.00

Payments

Date	Details	Receipt number	Cheque number	Amount
10 Jan	Rent of premises	5	1701	2500.00
11 Jan	Medical supplies	6	1702	3000.00
16 Jan	Purchase of drugs	7	1703	550.00
27 Jan	Office equipment	8	1704	100.00
				6150.00

(Difference: 7147.00 – 6150.00 = 997.00)

BANK STATEMENT/PASS BOOK

Date	Details	Debit	Credit	Balance
1 Jan	Balance brought forward			00.00
10 Jan	Sundries 856		7000.00	7000.00
10 Jan	Sundries 857		20.00	7020.00
14 Jan	Cheque 1702	3000.00		4020.00
19 Jan	Cheque 1703	550.00		3470.00
31 Jan	Charges	20.00		3450.00
31 Jan	Balance carried forward			3450.00

Figure 15: Example of bank book and bank statement/pass book

BANK RECONCILIATION STATEMENT AS AT ....

	Amount	Amount
Bank balance (from statement/pass book)		
Less: cheques not yet included in the bank's records	_____	_____
Plus: items paid in but not yet included in the bank's records	_____	_____
Balance in bank book		=======

Figure 16: Outline of a bank reconciliation statement

If you feel you need more practice at this, try to reconcile the bank book and statement/pass book shown in the example. It should look like Figure 17.

BANK RECONCILIATION STATEMENT AS AT 31 JANUARY 19___

	Amount	Amount
Bank balance (from statement/pass book)		3450.00
Less: cheques not yet included in the bank's records		
– cheque number 1701	2500.00	
– cheque number 1704	100.00	2600.00
		850.00
Plus: items paid in but not yet included in the bank's records		
– paying-in ref. 858	127.00	127.00
Balance in bank book		977.00

Figure 17: Bank reconciliation based on information in Figure 15

Comments on the reconciliation:

- The balance is 977.00, and not 997.00 as shown in the bank book (Figure 15), because the 20.00 for charges should be included on the payments side of your bank book.
- You may want to ask the bank why it has not yet credited the 127.00 to your account. (This was paid in on 12 January!)
- Cheque 1704 will, we assume, be included in the bank's records in early February.
- Cheque 1701 does not show up on the bank's records, because the person you gave it to has been slow in paying it into his/her account.
- Remember it may take up to a week (or more) for the bank to process the cheque you have written.

Rules to help you to control your bank account

There are rules which need to be observed when operating a bank account:

1 Whenever a bank account is opened, it should *always be registered in the name of the group*, never in the name of the leader or treasurer.
2 Arrange with your bank for all cheques written by your group to be *signed by two people*.
3 *Cheques should be used as much as possible* in making payments, as this avoids having to hold large amounts of cash on your premises. However, cheques are not always accepted as a method of payment. In this case you will have to pay in cash.
4 You should *never sign blank cheques*. Signed cheques are the equivalent of cash. If you really have no alternative, make sure that the name of the payee is included, and a limit set on the amount payable. Some banks will allow you to write this on the face of a cheque (for example, 'amount not to exceed two hundred ...').
5 Any money you receive should be *deposited into the bank as often as practical*. This is especially important over holidays and weekends, when surplus cash should not be left on the premises.
6 Cheques not cleared through the bank within a certain time-limit (six months in many countries) should be cancelled, and the payee should be contacted in case they have been lost.

Summary of this chapter

- There are different types of bank accounts: current, deposit, and savings.
- Open a bank book and enter in it everything that happens in the bank account.
- Use a separate page in the bank book for items going in (receipts) and items going out (payments).
- An analysed bank book will show you the type of payment made from the bank.
- You can combine the bank book and the cash book.
- When transfers of money are made between bank and cash, always remember to make an entry in both records.
- Agree your bank book with the bank's records regularly, by completing a bank reconciliation.
- A bank account should be kept in the name of the group, never in the name of an individual.
- Two people should always sign cheques or requests for money from the account.
- Do not sign blank cheques.
- Always pay money into the bank as soon as possible.

6 SUMMARISING THE ACCOUNTS

You are now able to complete your cash and bank books, and reconcile your bank statements. Next, you will want to summarise what you have received and what you have paid. This may be for your own use or for someone else. Whatever the reason, the next two chapters will show you how to do it.

Receipts

First, we look at the receipts recorded in the cash and bank books. This is shown in Figure 18.

CASH BOOK
Receipts

Date	Details	Receipt number	Amount
1 Jan	Cash in hand	—	1000.00
3 Jan	Grant from donor	500	9500.00
9 Jan	Grant from Dept. of Health	501	7000.00
9 Jan	Sale of drugs	502	14.50
	Total		17514.50

BANK BOOK
Receipts

Date	Details	Paying-in reference	Amount
10 Jan	Cash	856	7000.00
10 Jan	Sale of drugs	857	20.00
12 Jan	Sale of medical supplies	858	127.00
	Total		7147.00

Figure 18: Information from cash book and bank book receipts

All the items need to be summarised, apart from the 'Cash' received into the bank on 10 January. There should be a similar entry on the payments side of the cash book for 7000.00, described as 'Bank'. Overall, these two entries will cancel out, and neither needs to be included in the summary. This makes sense, as the only thing to change is *where* the money is held. It was cash, and now it's in the bank. There has been no new money received or paid. We can see from the information available that it refers to the 7000.00 received as a grant from the Department of Health on 9 January, which has now been paid into the bank. We have already included this item from the cash book in the summary.

In summarising the receipts, the categories we will use are:

• Grants received
• Sale of drugs
• Sale of medical supplies.

These categories should have *the same descriptions as those included in the budget*. The receipts summary will therefore look like Figure 19.

Receipts

Cash in hand 1 January	1000.00
Grants received	
– Donor	9500.00
– Dept. of Health	7000.00
Miscellaneous sales	161.50
Total receipts	17661.50

Figure 19: Summary of receipts

There are several points to note in this kind of summary:

• The 'cash in hand' figure is included as a 'receipt' of money, even though this is held at the beginning of the period. If there is a bank balance, this too must be included.
• If there are a number of grants, you could put in one figure to summarise them. However, it is better to list them separately, as donors like their names to be shown!

• The miscellaneous sales can include any number of items. If it is useful, you may show these separately.

(If you are using an analysed cash or bank book, you will realise that you can use the total at the bottom of each of the analysed columns as the figure to include in the summary.)

In reality, you are likely to have more items than are shown here, but the following rules apply whenever you summarise receipts:

• Start off with your opening cash and bank book balances.
• Summarise the accounts in the same order as the budget.
• Sub-divide the categories to give as much information as possible.

Payments

Now let us look at the summary of the payments. This is shown in Figure 20.

CASH BOOK
Payments

Date	Details	Receipt number	Amount
3 Jan	Stationery for office	1	10.00
5 Jan	Purchase of medical supplies	2	650.00
7 Jan	Driver's salary	3	200.00
7 Jan	Purchase of drugs	4	3450.00
10 Jan	Bank	–	7000.00
	Total		11310.00

BANK BOOK
Payments

Date	Details	Receipt number	Cheque number	Amount
10 Jan	Rent of premises	5	1701	2500.00
11 Jan	Medical supplies	6	1702	3000.00
16 Jan	Purchase of drugs	7	1703	550.00
27 Jan	Office equipment	8	1704	100.00
	Total			6150.00

Figure 20: Cash book and bank book payments

In this example no cheques have been written to obtain cash. If there were any, they would not be included in the summary of receipts and payments. This is because money is only being transferred from the bank account into cash. It is not involving anyone outside the group. It is important to remember this. Also, the 7000.00 paid from cash into the bank on 10 January is excluded, as it appears on the receipts side of the bank book, and therefore cancels it out.

The main categories of payment are:

• salaries
• rent of premises
• purchase of drugs
• purchase of medical supplies
• office equipment.

These are the same as the budget headings shown in Figure 1, except for the following points:

• There is a heading for 'Electricity', and nothing has yet been paid.
• There are no items for office equipment and stationery. But there is an item for 'Other expenses', so these costs will be entered there.
• Purchase of medical supplies is described as 'Other medical supplies', so this will be used here too.

The summary of payments would, therefore, look like Figure 21.

Payments	
Salaries	200.00
Rent of premises	2500.00
Purchase of drugs	4000.00
Other medical supplies	3650.00
Electricity	—
Other expenses	
– office equipment	100.00
– office stationery	10.00
Total payments	10460.00
Cash/bank balance in	
hand 31 January	2554.50
	13014.50

Figure 21: Summary of payments

You will see that the payments summary has a figure included for cash in hand (described here as cash/bank balance) on 31 January. This should agree with the amount of cash held at that date, plus the balance in the bank book (which has been agreed with the bank statement or pass book). This will be used as the opening 'cash in hand' figure in your next month's accounts.

With this balance included, the total of the receipts and the total of the payments now agree. This kind of summary is called a **receipts and payments account**. It summarises what has happened to your cash and bank items, and gives an overall picture of what you have received and paid.

Whenever this kind of summary is used, the heading will say that it is a receipts and payments account, and it will state the name of the group or project involved, and the period of time that it covers.

Putting it all together

Figure 22 gives a presentation of the whole account.

RECEIPTS AND PAYMENTS ACCOUNT FOR THE PRIMARY HEALTH CARE
PROJECT FOR THE PERIOD 1 TO 31 JANUARY 19–

Receipts			Payments	
Cash in hand 1 Jan		1000.00	Salaries	200.00
			Rent of premises	2500.00
Grants received			Purchase of drugs	4000.00
– Donor	9500.00		Other medical supplies	3650.00
– Dept. of Health	7000.00	16500.00	Electricity	–
			Other expenses	
Miscellaneous sales		161.50	– office equipment	100.00
			– office stationery	10.00
				10460.00
			Cash/bank balance in hand 31 Jan	7201.50
		17661.50		17661.50

Figure 22: Example of a receipts and payments account

Receipts and payments accounts should always be presented with the same main headings as in your budget. This makes comparisons easier, as we will see in a later chapter. Also, make sure that the totals are underlined (as shown above: 17661.50).

Summary of this chapter

- One way of summarising your accounts is to use a receipts and payments account.
- If items are paid into the bank account from the cash book, exclude them from the summary. Remember this when cash is withdrawn from the bank.
- Summarise the receipts and the payments under the same headings as used in the budget.
- If the heading covers different items, sub-divide these to give more information.
- Include the cash/bank book balances at the beginning and end of the period covered.
- The 'balancing' figures at the bottom of the receipts side and the payments side must be the same. Write them down and underline the figures.
- Remember to give the summary a title: Receipts and Payments Account, and state the name of the group or project, and the period covered.

7 SUMMARISING YOUR ACCOUNTS IN MORE DETAIL

The last chapter showed how to put together a receipts and payments account. This is a useful way of summarising all the money that has come in and gone out. However, there are some limitations to this way of working. This chapter will show you a number of steps to improve the usefulness of the receipts and payments account.

How to improve the receipts and payments account

Amounts paid in advance, or owed by you

The receipts and payments account gives you a summary of all items. It does not tell you how much relates to a specific period of time. For example, if the electricity charge for January were paid in February, it would not appear in the January account, so it would look as though no electricity had been used. There are two ways of avoiding this:

- Try to avoid having items outstanding at the end of a month! In practice this is not easy, but as far as possible you should keep amounts to the minimum by paying invoices for the period before the date at which you prepare the receipts and payments account.
- Keep a record of which items are outstanding at the end of a period, and include the total for that budget item as a note at the bottom of the receipts and payments account.

Saving money to replace items that will wear out

It is important to save for the eventual replacement of items such as equipment, vehicles, or machinery. Each month, put aside some money towards the cost of replacing each item. Pay this into a savings or deposit account. Any interest gained can be added to the account. It will be shown as a payment out of your current account bank book, and as a receipt into your savings or deposit account bank book. In the receipts and payments account it will appear as a payment, but a note at the bottom of the account should show that this account is for replacements.

How much should you set aside each month? You could divide up the cost of the item by the number of months it is likely to last. For example, you could say that a typewriter which originally cost 480.00 will last four years. So you would put 10.00 per month (480.00 divided by 48 months) into an account for each of the four years.

However, with ever-increasing prices, it is likely that in four years' time a typewriter will cost much more than 480.00, and you would not have enough money to replace it. The amount to be set aside each month depends on the circumstances, the life of the item, the rate of inflation, and the exchange rate (for purchases overseas). As a guide, an amount based on *double the original cost* may be appropriate.

Your group may feel it is not possible to put money aside in this way. If so, you need to ask yourself what will happen when the item is no longer usable. You may feel that the only way to replace it would be to ask for a further grant or arrange additional fundraising. If the future of the group depends on the item, arrangements should be made well in advance, and not left until it is useless.

Separating longer-term items from day-to-day expenses

The receipts and payments account treats all expenditure in the same way. It will not be obvious in the summary if a large amount has been spent on items that you intend to keep for a long time, such as equipment or machinery. (Such items are sometimes called **fixed assets**.) So you should make a note of such purchases at the end of the account, as shown in Figure 23.

Fixed assets bought during the year:

	Cost
Office equipment	890.00
Machinery	1655.00
Total	2545.00

Figure 23: A record of fixed assets appended to a receipts and payments account

Has a surplus been made?

The receipts and payments account may show how you are doing in terms of cash or bank balance available, but not whether you have made a profit or a loss. If you need to find this out, a further account summary should be prepared. You may need the help of a professional accountant to do this.

You may like to look back at the receipts and payments account that we put together in the last chapter (Figure 22), and see what notes might have been added there to make the information clearer. The notes needed for this example are added to the summary shown in the next chapter (Figure 24).

An additional example of a receipts and payments account, with notes, is shown in Appendix 1.

Summary of this chapter

- Try to avoid amounts being paid in advance or owed.
- Keep a list of any items outstanding at the date of your receipts and payments summary, and include a note of these at the end of the account.
- It is important to set aside money for the eventual replacement of longer-term items.
- This money should be put into a savings or deposit account each month.
- The calculation of how much this should be will depend on the inflation and exchange rates and the life of the item.
- Show in a note how much has been spent on items with a relatively long life.
- The receipts and payments account will show you the cash/bank position, but not the profit or loss you have made.

Although the receipts and payments account and the advice given here will help with all accounting, when a project starts to grow (when it has a number of employees, and owns vehicles and equipment), it will need to produce a more advanced financial summary. Such accounts are outside the scope of this book, and further help should be sought from an accountant if it is needed.

8 PROVIDING THE INFORMATION THAT YOUR GROUP NEEDS

One of the reasons for accounting is to keep an accurate record of the financial activities of a group or project. Another is to be able to use this information to manage and improve the project. Good use of financial information is often the key to a project's success or failure.

Often queries will arise, and the cash and bank books will help to answer them. Start there, and if the entry in the book itself does not help, the references will tell you where to find more information.

How much money is left?

The cash book will tell you if you have enough money to pay your expenses. You need to look at this constantly to make sure that you do not run out of cash. Likewise, the bank book will show what is left in the bank account. If you are likely to run out of money altogether, you must alert the people responsible for running the group or project as soon as possible. If this is not done, the whole project could be in danger of failing.

Regular reporting

When we looked at budgeting (in Chapter 2), we said that in addition to making the overall budget, it was also helpful to divide it up, showing what money would be available month by month (Figure 2).

Looking again at our example of a primary health care project, we will prepare a summary for January, including the transfer to a savings account for the eventual replacement of medical equipment (explained in Chapter 7). This is referred to as a **budget and actual statement**, and uses the same headings as the budget. See Figure 24.

BUDGET AND ACTUAL STATEMENT FOR THE MONTH OF JANUARY 19—

Item	Note	Budgeted amount for January	Amount rec'd/ spent in January	Difference
RECEIPTS				
Grants received				
– Donor		9500.00	9500.00	0.00
– Dept. of Health	1	14000.00	7000.00	(7000.00)
Miscellaneous sales		50.00	161.50	111.50
Total receipts		23550.00	16661.50	(6888.50)
PAYMENTS				
Salaries		1000.00	200.00	800.00
Rent of premises	2	417.00	2500.00	(2083.00)
Purchase of drugs		5000.00	4000.00	1000.00
Other medical supplies	3	4400.00	3650.00	750.00
Electricity	4	83.00	–	83.00
Transfer to savings account	5	–	70.00	(70.00)
Other expenses		167.00	110.00	57.00
Total payments		11067.00	10530.00	537.00
Total difference		12483.00	6131.50	(6351.50)

Notes:

1 **The Department of Health** grant was to have been paid in two halves; it will now be paid quarterly.

2 **Rent of premises** has been paid in January for the six months from January to June.

3 **Other medical supplies**: These include fixed assets bought during January:

	Cost
Medical equipment	1250.00
	1250.00

4 **Electricity** is due to be paid in March. It is estimated that 95.00 is owed for January.

5 **Amounts held in cash/bank**

	Amount
Balance held in cash 31 Jan.	547.50
Balance in current account 31 Jan.	6584.00
Balance held in savings account (for medical equipment) 31 Jan.	70.00
Total	7201.50

6 **Amounts in brackets** () show negative differences.

Figure 24: Example of a budget and actual statement

Notes like those needed at the end of the receipts and payment account (explained in Chapter 7) are included here, to give more information.

This type of report with its regular breakdown gives an overall picture of the group's finances, and will be needed by group members, or the management committee.

What does the statement show?

- It shows that you have received considerably less than expected in the budget, mainly because the Department of Health grant is now coming in four parts, rather than two. This could be disastrous for the project, but looking at the figures, it seems that the money was not all needed in January. You will need to consult and amend the cash flow forecast to see what effect this will have on future months.
- Rent paid in January for six months in advance means that the project may run short of cash. Again, consult the cash flow forecast.
- The medical equipment is a long-term item, and may not have been budgeted. If so, less money will be available for other medical supplies, and a decision will have been made about what is the highest priority. All long-term items should be shown separately in the budget.
- As the item of equipment has been purchased in January, this is the first month that a transfer has been made to a savings account. As the date for the replacement of the item draws nearer (perhaps a number of years yet), you will be able to see exactly what is available to replace it.

  You will notice that the total amount of money held, shown in note 5, is the same as that in Figure 22. The only difference is the breakdown.

  No amount has been included in the budget for transfer to a savings account. This needs to be added. Indeed, whenever fixed assets are to be bought, the budget should include a transfer to pay for their eventual replacement.

- Showing negative variances in brackets helps to draw people's attention to the figures that may cause concern.
- One of the reasons for overspending may be that prices have increased. If this is the case for a specific item, or if the increase distorts the figures, it is important to draw attention to this in a

note saying what has happened.

- Always look closely at what has actually happened, and keep asking questions. If there is a difference, always check whether it has been caused by timing (if receipts have come in or payments have gone out earlier or later than you had planned), or whether it is something that you had not planned at all. If so, what will you do about it?
- This monthly report will be of vital importance when your organisation takes policy decisions, so be sure that the information is as accurate and up to date as possible.
- A column for the percentage difference between the 'budget' and 'actual' figures could be added to highlight major variations.

It is very important to produce a summary like this regularly, so that everyone can see the financial situation.

In addition to the monthly report shown in Figure 24, it is useful to present a report for the months from the beginning of the financial year to date. Of course in January, or whenever your year starts, there would be only one month to report on. The headings for such a report at the end of March would look like Figure 25.

Item	Budget Mar	Amt recd/ spent: Mar	Difference	Budget Jan-Mar	Amt recd/ spent: Jan-Mar	Difference

Figure 25: Headings for a cumulative budget and actual statement

Reporting to people who have given you money

A financial report will normally be sent regularly (usually every six months) to organisations which have given you money. This should include

- the receipts and payments account for the period to which the amount relates;
- the cumulative budget and actual statement;

- details of how the individual donation has been spent, if it was given for a particular purpose; and if any money is left over, a note to say how much;
- an explanation of any changes to this year's budget;
- a budget for next year, if appropriate.

Summary of this chapter

- The information in the accounts is important to the running of any group.
- Make use of the cash book and bank book to answer queries.
- Know how much money you have left in cash and/or at the bank.
- Present your budget and actual statement regularly to the people or group responsible for running the project.
- Add notes to this to give more information.
- Include a similar report from the beginning of the year to date (a cumulative budget and actual statement).
- Be critical, and keep asking questions about anything in the statement that you do not understand.
- Send regular reports to the people who have given you money.

9 HAVING THE ACCOUNTS CHECKED

The work of the person keeping a group's accounts must always be checked by another person at least once a year. This is so that mistakes can be found and corrected, and that the person who is keeping the account can prove that s/he is honest. This type of check is called an **audit**, and the person carrying it out is called an **auditor**.

Who is appointed as auditor?

The most important fact about the person who is appointed as auditor is that he or she is independent. The auditor must not be involved in the keeping of the accounts, or be related to any of the group leaders. The person should be respected, and able to communicate with people well. S/he should have some knowledge of book-keeping, and ideally be a qualified accountant. In some countries this is a legal requirement. The auditor may require a fee or payment. Do not forget to include this in your budget!

What happens when an audit takes place?

The audit will usually take place once a year, soon after the end of the period covered by your accounts. The auditor will want to count your cash, and see the following records:

- cash and bank books
- receipts for money coming in and payments going out
- invoices
- any correspondence about the project, and especially about the accounting

- bank statements or pass books
- cheque books and old cheque stubs, paying-in slips/books
- bank reconciliations
- budget and actual statements
- receipts and payments account
- a record of any group meetings.

The auditor will examine these and other documents in detail, and will ask questions to clarify the information in it. S/he will also ask for information about the way in which the group is run.

After the audit, the auditor will usually write to the leader of the group or to the management committee to say what has been done (this is called a **management letter**). The letter may suggest ways to improve the accounts and the project management as a whole. This is very useful, and it can help you to make your project more successful. When all this has been done, the auditor will 'sign your accounts' (usually a copy of the receipts and payments account) to say they are correct. Copies of this can then be sent to anyone who is interested.

Other audits

In addition to the annual audit, other people may want to have a look at your accounts for themselves. Anyone who has given you money for your project has the right to do this, and it is good practice to welcome them. It will help to maintain a good relationship with people who are likely to give you money in the future! In reality, however, if an audit has already been carried out, many people will be happy to accept a copy of the receipts and payments account signed by the auditor.

Summary of this chapter

- An independent auditor must be appointed to check the accounts.
- S/he should have some knowledge of book-keeping, or be a qualified accountant.
- The audit should take place soon after the period covered by your accounts, and all records will be inspected.
- A management letter will be written, with recommendations for improving the financial management of the project.
- The receipts and payments account should be signed to say that the audit has taken place.
- Other people may want to audit your accounts. Welcome them!

APPENDIX 1: EXAMPLE OF A RECEIPTS AND PAYMENTS ACCOUNT

(An alternative layout to that shown in Figure 22)

Lomtaka Community Group: Training Centre Project
Annual Receipts and Payments Account for the period 1 April 19— to
31 March 19—

Last year's amount		Note	Amount	Amount
3687	Cash in hand (Cash/bank) 1 April 19—			8946
	Receipts			
–	Development grant	1	6000	
31329	Donations	2	31365	
25468	Fees for courses	3	34751	
56797	Total receipts			72116
60484				81062
	Payments			
–	Purchase of training equipment	4	6155	
–	Transfer to savings account	5	1862	
33125	Salaries		40028	
6205	Training materials		8759	
3520	Travel costs		3812	
5933	Rent of centre	6	7780	
902	Electricity	7	861	
296	Water charge	6	396	
	Office costs			
450	– telephone	8	572	
1045	– printing, postage, stationery		959	
62	– bank charges		104	
51538	Total payments			71288
8946	Cash in hand (cash/bank) 31 March 19—	9		9774

Notes to the account:

1 **The development grant** was given by the Education Department for the purchase of new training equipment (see also note 3).

2 **Donations** received from:

	Amount
Training Development Trust	5000
Co-operative Skills Association	11365
Rural Training Fund	15000
Total	31365

3 **Fees for courses** include 810.00 paid in advance for a course in June 19—.

4 **Purchase of fixed assets** (training equipment):

	Cost
Projector and screen	4257
Tape recorder	1898
Total	6155

5 **Amounts transferred to savings account** are for eventual replacement of projector and screen and tape recorder.

6 **Rent of centre and water charges** cover the period 1 April 19— to 31 March 19—.

7 **Electricity** paid is for 11 months (April to February). It is estimated that the March charge will be 75.00, payable in June.

8 **Telephone** payment includes a payment of 35.00 for two months' rental in advance.

9 **Breakdown of cash/bank amounts** held at 31 March 19—:

	Amount
Balance in cash	648
Balance in current account	1894
Balance in deposit account	5370
Balance in savings account:	
– replacement of projector and screen	1288
– replacement of tape recorder	574
Total	9774

APPENDIX 2:
GLOSSARY OF TERMS USED

Accountant: Someone who is qualified (usually by taking exams) to give financial advice.

Accounting: The method of recording and using information to prepare financial summaries/statements and reports.

Accounts: The records kept and statements produced to show how a group has used its money.

Analysed cash book: The record of all cash (and or bank amounts) coming in and going out, with additional columns to identify the type of receipt or payment. (See Chapter 4.)

Audit: An independent assessment of a group's accounts and other records. (See Chapter 9.)

Auditor: A person who carries out an audit. (See Chapter 9.)

Balance brought forward (or **balance b/f):** an amount of money that is included in the cash book, bank book, or other record as a starting point at the beginning of a new accounting period. The same figure would have been shown as a balance carried forward, at the end of the previous period. This term is also used for the balance at the start of a page.

Balance carried forward (or **balance c/f):** A figure included in the accounts as an amount remaining at the end of an accounting period. This will be the same as the balance brought forward in the next period. This term is also used for the balance at the end of a page.

Bank book: A record kept by the group itself, showing all items going in or out of the bank account. (See Chapter 5.)

Bank charge: A charge made for operating a bank account.

Bank pass book: A book provided and updated by the bank to show the record of money in an account. (See Chapter 5.)

Bank reconciliation: A way of confirming that a group's own accounting records agree with those of the bank. (See Chapter 5.)

Bank statement: A list produced by a bank, showing all entries in an account over a period of time, and the balance held at the end of that period. (See Chapter 5.)

Book-keeper: A person who keeps records of accounts.

Budget: A financial summary of a plan relating to a period of time. (See Chapter 2.)

Budget and actual statement: A report which compares budgeted and actual receipts and payments. (See Chapter 8.)

Cash book: A record of all cash coming in and going out. (See Chapter 3.)

Cash flow forecast (or **cash budget**): A way of stating, in advance, what money is expected to come in and go out of a project over a fixed period of time. (See Chapter 2.)

Cash in hand: The amount of money held. Can refer to cash, or to the total of cash and bank amounts.

Cheque: A document provided by a bank to enable you to draw money from your bank account.

Cumulative total: The total for the current period added to the total for previous periods.

Current account: A type of bank account into which money can be paid, and from which cheques can be written and money withdrawn. (See Chapter 5.)

Deposit account: A bank account that gains interest. The bank may require a number of days' advance notice to withdraw funds. (See Chapter 5.)

Expenditure: Costs which have been paid.

Fixed assets: Items that are kept for more than one year, for example vehicles and equipment.

Income receipt: A piece of paper that gives details of an amount of money received, and the signature of the person receiving the money. (See Chapter 3.)

Inflation: Term used to refer to an increase in prices.

Interest: Money added to your money when it is held by someone else, for example, a bank.

Invoice: A written request for payment.

Management committee: People who are (legally) responsible for the running of a group.

Management letter: Report sent to the group's leader or management committee at the end of an audit.

Objectives: A summary of future plans.

Overdraft: An amount that a bank allows to be temporarily overspent from your account.

Paying-in slip/book: A document provided by a bank to enable you to pay money into your account.

Payment: Money given to someone else for the provision of goods or services.

Payment receipt: A piece of paper that gives details of an amount paid, and the signature of the person who has received the money. (See Chapter 3.)

Receipt: Money coming in; or a piece of paper acknowledging money received or pay-ment made.

Receipts and payments account: A summary of bank and cash items coming in and going out of a group over a period of time. (See Chapter 6.)

Reconciliation: A means of agreeing one part of the accounts with another.

Savings account: Bank account that gives interest and is intended for money that is not required for some time. May also be called an **investment account**, and is sometimes the same as a deposit account.

Treasurer: The person who keep records of accounts.

APPENDIX 3: SOME BLANK FORMS WHICH YOU MAY FIND USEFUL

BUDGET FOR PERIOD _____ TO _____

Item	Jan	Feb	Mar	Apr	May	Jun	July	Aug	Sept	Oct	Nov	Dec	Total
Money coming in													
Total													
Cumulative total													
Money going out													
Total													
Cumulative total													

ANALYSED CASH BOOK

Budget headings

Date	Details	Receipt number	Amount					
	Total							

This form could be used for receipts or payments

Bank reconciliation as at...

	Amount	Amount

Bank balance (from statement/pass book)

Less: cheques not yet included
in the bank's records
cheque number

Plus: items paid in but not yet
included in the bank's records
paying-in reference

Balance in bank book

A bank reconciliation statement

BUDGET AND ACTUAL EXPENDITURE STATEMENT UP TO
THE MONTH OF ....19........

Item	Note	MONTH......................			CUMULATIVE (from.........to.......)		
		Budgeted amount	Amount spent	Difference	Budgeted amount	Amount spent	Difference

Receipts

Total receipts

Payments

Total payments

Total difference

56

Last year's amount	RECEIPTS AND PAYMENTS ACCOUNT FOR THE PERIOD....................TO	Note	Amount	Amount
	Cash in hand			
	Receipts			
	Payments			
	Cash in hand			

FURTHER READING

D.E.N. Dickson (ed.): *Improve Your Business: Handbook*, Geneva: International Labour Office, 1986.

Manual on Financial Management and Accounts Keeping, New Delhi: Society for Participatory Research in Asia (PRIA), 1991.
(Includes a good summary of the Indian Foreign Contributions Act.)

E. Millard: *Financial Management of a Small Handicraft Business*, Oxford: Oxfam / London: Intermediate Technology Publications, 1987.

F. Vincent: *Manual of Practical Management for Third World Rural Development Associations, Volume II: Financial Management*, Geneva: IRED, 1989.

Other books on financial management from Oxfam Publications

Basic Accounting for Credit and Savings Schemes
Nicola Elliott

A simple and practical guide which assumes no previous knowledge of accounting, and explains all the principles and tasks relevant to financial management. Useful as a general introduction to basic accounting, and also to credit control and stock control.

The author was formerly Senior International Accountant at Oxfam (UK and Ireland) and is now Head of Accounts at Voluntary Service Overseas (VSO).

ISBN 0 85598 275 6
1996

The Financial Management of a Small Handicraft Business
Edward Millard

A short book which explains the basic financial concepts involved in the effective planning of day-to-day operations, to help small businesses to plan their working capital requirements and achieve profitability.

The author worked for many years as a trainer and marketing manager with Oxfam Trading.

ISBN 0 85598 082 6
1988

For a copy of the Oxfam Publications catalogue or for further information, please contact Oxfam Publishing, 274 Banbury Road, Oxford OX2 7DZ, UK. Fax: +44 (0)1865 313925; e-mail publish@oxfam.org.uk